Four Square (4□)
for Writing Assessment
Elementary Level

Written by Judith S. Gould and Mary F. Burke

Cover and book designed by Kati Baker

Teaching & Learning Company

a Lorenz company
P.O. Box 802
Dayton, OH 45401-0802
www.LorenzEducationalPress.com

This book belongs to

_____

TLC105

Table of Contents

Preface

There are many different ways to start a piece of writing. Some dig right in and create a first draft without any formal pre-writing. Others web, outline, draw, or otherwise plan their writing before beginning a first draft. We've witnessed writers using sticky notes and random paper scraps and other writers sit in silent meditation before putting pencil to paper. The truth is that all of these methods are the right way to start a piece of writing.

When it comes to the writing assessment, however, we often do not have time for the flexible approaches that work well in the collaborative environment of the writing classroom. On assessment day, we cannot confer with students, and students cannot assist one another. The writer must have a method to deliver their best writing on demand. That writing needs to be organized, focused, detailed, and engaging. The writer needs a plan on assessment day, and we believe that the Four Square plan is the best way to get the job done.

The Four Square was designed to be a starting place for writing. Using the Four Square tool will help writers organize and brainstorm in a hurry, allowing for the time and attention that well crafted, detailed writing deserves. Once the initial draft is completed, writers need concrete strategies to do the work of reviewing and revising the writing. The three-step revision method is flexible yet concrete. Provide your writers with the tools they need, practice using them, and you are on your way to assessment success!

TLC105

Learning the Four Square for Informational Writing

Reminders

Here are some reminders before you begin. Four Square...

- is a tool, a web on folded paper
- strengthens structure, which helps with organization and memory
- is a map for ideas, words and phrases
- can be used with all language levels, from emerging to proficient
- is great for visual learners
- begins with folding paper into four squares

Prepare

- ☐ a piece of chart paper
- ☐ colored markers
- ☐ a piece of loose-leaf paper (or grade-appropriate paper) for each of the students

Getting Started

Say to the students, "Sometimes getting started is the hardest part of writing. Today we are going to learn something that will help us get started in our writing." Tell the students you are going to learn how to use a Four Square. "When you go on a trip, you need a map because it shows you the way to go. A Four Square is like a map or set of directions for the ideas and thoughts you have for writing."

Illustrations

Get out the chart paper and fold it in front of the kids. To make a Four Square, you need to make two hamburger folds (or you could do a hot dog and a hamburger) on the paper. Open it up—what do you see? Now you know where the name *Four Square* came from!

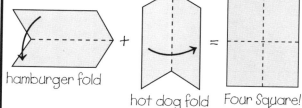

hamburger fold + hot dog fold = Four Square!

Student Task Have the students fold their own papers. Assist where needed. Instruct the students to unfold their papers and draw a box in the middle of their Four Squares, as shown. Check students' work before moving on.

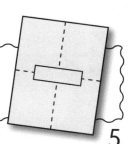

Brainstorming Using a Four Square

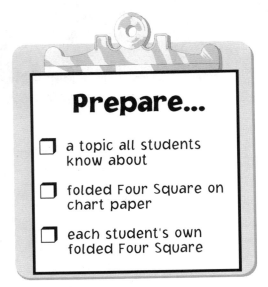

Prepare...

☐ a topic all students know about

☐ folded Four Square on chart paper

☐ each student's own folded Four Square

Here are a few ideas for student topics:

My favorite food is...
Recess is fun!
My pet is my best friend

Choose a topic to demonstrate in front of the class. With a colored marker, model writing the topic in the middle box. The topic used throughout the example given is *Recess is fun!* Remind students that the topic is what they will be writing about.

Recess is fun!

Student Task Have the students fill in the middle squares of their Four Squares. Check before moving on.

Recess is fun!

Show the students that there are four squares in which to put ideas. You want to put different ideas in **three** of the squares that relate to the topic. Some ideas may include *going on the swings*, *playing on the monkey bars*, and *playing tag*. Volunteer some non-examples, like *eating pizza* or *taking care of my baby brother*, to illustrate the importance of staying on topic.

On your chart, choose one idea to write in the upper-left square of the Four Square. Write the idea at the top of the square. Show the students how to write the first idea as a short phrase and not as a complete sentence. For example, you would write *going on the swings* instead of *I like going on the swings when I am on the playground*. Explain that since the Four Square is a map or plan, they can write in phrases to help them remember what the complete sentence will be.

Student Task

Have the students add the first idea to their Four Square. Check before moving on.

Repeat this step in the upper-right and lower-left squares of the Four Square. You should have three main ideas (*going on the swings*, *playing on the monkey bars*, and *playing tag*) in these three squares.

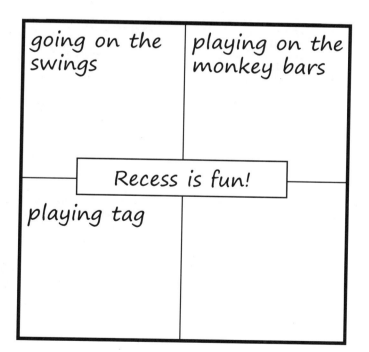

Student Task

Have the students fill in these squares on their own Four Squares. Check before moving on.

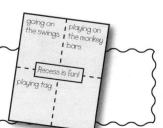

Filling in the Details — First Square

Point to the first square that says *going on the swings*, and tell the students that the square needs more ideas if it's going to be a strong paragraph. Ask the students what more they can tell you about enjoying the swings during recess.

Tell the students that these are called **supporting details**. Supporting details tell more about the main idea of the square. Accept the details that are interesting, and praise the use of strong verbs and adjectives to support the main idea. (Again, you may want to volunteer some non-examples to reinforce the idea of staying focused. *Hanging upside down on the pull up bars may* be on the topic of *recess is fun*, but not in the *going on the swings* main idea square.)

Prompt the students with questions such as:

Who plays with you?
Do you like to push or swing?
What does it feel like when you swing up high?
What do you see up there?

You may get responses such as:

my friend pushes me
like to go higher and higher
sometimes I jump off

Write the supporting details in bulleted form in the main idea square marked *going on the swings*.

going on the swings

• my friend Judy pushes me

• like to go higher and higher

• sometimes I jump off

Remind the students that these short phrases are not sentences, but only sentence holders. These sentence holders are there to remind the students what to include so they don't have to worry about forgetting their good ideas!

Point to each supporting detail that is now written in the first main idea square. Ask students to give you nice, juicy sentences based on these details. Remind them that these sentences will be part of the paragraph. Once again, show them how writing the short phrases will easily allow them to go back to complete sentences.

Have the students add details to their first squares. Check before moving on.

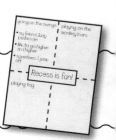

TLC105

Filling in the Details — Second Square

Point to the upper-right square of the Four Square. Tell the students you are now going to think of details to put in the main idea square marked *playing on the monkey bars.* Ask them to come up with some ideas for the details.

Prompt them with questions such as:

What do the monkey bars look like?

Who do you like to play with?

How do you play?

Where on the monkey bars do you play?

The students may come up with a variety of responses. Chart the ones that use the best descriptive language and tell the students your reasons. For example, you may say, "I'm going to include Suzie's detail of 'swinging across, hand over hand, on the top ladder with legs flying' because I can see it in my mind."

Add all the details for the *monkey bars* paragraph to the second square.

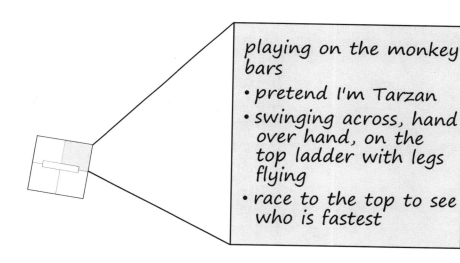

playing on the monkey bars
- pretend I'm Tarzan
- swinging across, hand over hand, on the top ladder with legs flying
- race to the top to see who is fastest

Point to each supporting detail in the square and ask students to give you nice, juicy sentences. Show them again how writing the short phrases will easily allow them to go back to full sentences.

Student Task

Ask the students to add details to their second squares. Check before moving on.

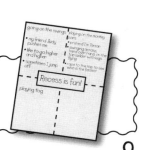

Filling in the Details — Third Square

SAY & DO

Point to the lower-left square of the Four Square. Tell the students you are now going to think of details to put in the main idea square marked *playing tag*. Ask them to come up with some ideas for the details.

Prompt them with questions such as:
What kind of tag do you play?
What are the rules?
Who do you like to play with?
Where are the boundaries?
Who is the best at IT?

The students may come up with a variety of responses. Chart the ones that use the best descriptive language and tell the students your reasons. For example, you may say, "I'm going to include Tommy's detail of 'playing freeze tag between the soccer goal and the monkey bars' because it gives me a good description in my mind of where tag takes place during recess."

Continue to add the details to the square that support the main idea *playing tag*.

playing tag
• playing freeze tag between the soccer goal and the monkey bars
• sometimes play in partners
• had to outrun Tommy, who is the fastest runner

Point to each supporting detail in the square and ask students to give you nice, juicy sentences. Show them again how writing the short phrases will easily allow them to go back to full sentences.

Student Task

Have the students add details to their third squares. The fourth square should remain empty. Check before moving on.

Adding Transitions Using a Four Square

Transitional devices indicate an organized thought pattern. When transitions exist in a piece of writing, the reader can easily move from one idea to the next without confusion. Transitional devices are also one indicator that is almost always named on scoring rubrics for writing assessments, so we want to be sure our students have them in their writing!

At the start of writing time, show your students the puzzle. Ask if anyone has done a puzzle and can explain how puzzles work. Invite a student or two to come to the front and complete the puzzle. As they are settling in for this "puzzling" writing lesson, take one puzzle piece and snip off one "nub." Guaranteed moans and groans from your students!

Prepare...

- ☐ an old puzzle, or pick up a small jigsaw puzzle at a discount store
- ☐ scissors
- ☐ copies of **Connecting Words** sheet (page 12)

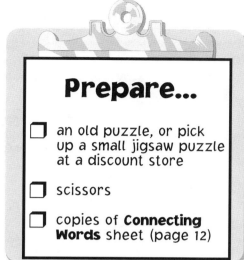

✦ First of all
    going on the swings

- my friend Judy pushes me
- like to go higher and higher
- sometimes I jump off

✦ Also
    playing on the monkey bars

- pretend I'm Tarzan
- swinging across, hand over hand, on the top ladder with legs flying
- race to the top to see who is fastest

Recess is fun!

✦ Finally
    playing tag

- playing freeze tag between the soccer goal and the monkey bars
- sometimes play in partners
- had to outrun Tommy, who is the fastest runner

✦ So you can see

Call on a student to explain why the puzzle won't work. Writing without "nubs" doesn't work either. We need something to **hold our ideas together**. Writers use words to do this.

On the chart paper where you modeled your Four Square, draw a puzzle piece in the upper-left corner of each of the four squares.

Show students the puzzle piece **Connecting Words** page. Call on students to choose words to place in your Four Square.

 Student Task

Have students draw puzzle pieces and write the appropriate words in their own Four Squares. Reminder—the puzzle pieces do not need to be gorgeous! After students have finished, check to make sure that they chose the appropriate words for each section of their Four Square.

Connecting Words

First of all
To start with
First
First of all
One thought
One reason
One thing
The first thing that comes
to mind is
Initially

Also
In addition
Additionally
Another thought
Another reason
Another thing
Second

Also
In addition
Additionally
Another thought
Another reason
Another thing
Third
Finally

So you can see
As one can see
In summary
In conclusion
Therefore
All in all
Thus

12

Adding Vivid Vocabulary

Look at the first main idea square marked *going on the swings*.

Tell the students that it's a good idea to try to add interesting or descriptive words to each square. This way, they can remember to use the words when they are writing their paragraphs.

Example:

In an oval, add the phrase *bigger than me* next to *Judy*. In another oval, add the word *sail*, which is a more descriptive word than *go*.

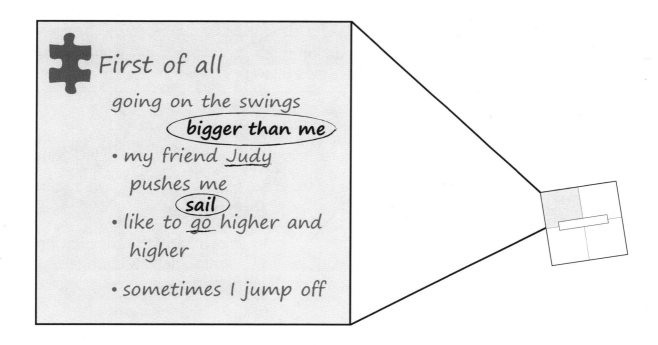

When students add vivid vocabulary in the planning stages, it's a bit of an early revision which can save time and energy.

Look at the main idea square marked *playing on monkey bars*.

Tell the students that you're going to add interesting or descriptive words to this square, too. Let them know that this will help them remember to use the words when they are writing their paragraphs.

Example:

In an oval, add *"AHHHYYYEEE!"* by the word *Tarzan*, which adds some interesting dialogue.

> **Also**
>
> playing on the monkey bars **"AHHHYYYEEE!"**
> - pretend I'm <u>Tarzan</u>
> - swinging across, hand over hand, on the top ladder with legs flying
> - race to the top to see who is fastest

When students add a little bit of dialogue, it can add a lot of interest to their writing as long as it's done with purpose. A little dialogue goes a long way! It's not to be overused.

Look at the main idea square marked *playing tag*.

Tell the students that you're going to add interesting or descriptive words to this square as well. This will help students remember to use the words when they are writing their paragraphs.

> **Finally**
>
> playing tag
> - playing freeze tag between the soccer goal and the monkey bars
> - sometimes play in partners
> - had to outrun Tommy, who is the *swiftest* <u>fastest</u> runner

Example:

In an oval, add the word *swiftest* next to *Tommy*. That's a stronger synonym for *fastest*.

Student Task

Have the students add vivid vocabulary to their plans.

14

TLC105

Developing an Ending Using a Four Square

Point to the blank square of the Four Square. Tell the students that this is the square for their endings.

Tell the students that informational writing needs to have an ending. The ending doesn't give more details, but sometimes ends with a personal feeling. Sometimes it can end with a question that serves as an invitation to the reader. Other times it can end looking back and summarizing the main ideas. Write these three endings on the board:

> • Recess is my favorite time of day. I never get tired of going outside to play!
>
> • Recess is such fun! Wouldn't you like to come out with my friends and me when we play?
>
> • Recess is the greatest because of the high-flying swings, the acrobatic monkey bars and the excitement of playing tag. Let's go now!

Explain that the first ending is called a *personal feelings ending*. In this case, the personal feelings ending tells the reader how the author feels about recess. This ending is by far the easiest ending to write, because anyone can tell how he or she feels about a topic.

The second ending is an *invitation* or *question ending*. It invites the reader to share the feeling of the topic.

The third ending is a *summary ending*. This type of ending restates the main ideas.

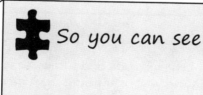

So you can see

Recess is my favorite time of the day. I never get tired of going outside to play!

Most times, you can use a combination of the three endings for a satisfying sense of closure to most informational pieces. Of course, there are many other ways to end a piece of informational writing. These three are the easiest to access for most students.

Student Task

Now have students create their own endings!

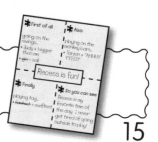

Example Four Square Paragraphs

 **First of all**

going on the swings
(bigger than me)
- my friend <u>Judy</u> pushes <u>me</u>
(sail)
- like to <u>go</u> higher and higher

- sometimes I jump off

 Also

playing on the <u>monkey</u> bars   ("AHHHYYYEEE!")
- pretend I'm <u>Tarzan</u>
- swinging across, hand over hand, on the top ladder with legs flying
- race to the top to see who is fastest

Recess is fun!

 **Finally**

playing tag
- playing freeze tag between the soccer goal and the monkey bars
- sometimes play in partners
- had to outrun Tommy, who is the (swiftest) <u>fastest runner</u>

 So you can see

Recess is my favorite time of the day. I never get tired of going outside to play!

Recess is fun!

First of all, playing on the swings is the best. My friend Judy and I take turns on the swings. She's bigger than I am, so she pushes me way up high. The wind whooshes past my face and sometimes I see birds flying by me. When my turn ends, I jump off in mid-air and land in the dirt in a cloud of dust.

Also, the monkey bars are always lots of fun. I like to pretend I'm Tarzan and give that yell, "AHHHHHHHH-HHYYYYYYYYEEEEEEEEEE!" I swing hand over hand across the top of the overhanging ladder and imagine I'm swinging over a rushing river. Sometimes my friends and I race all the way to the top of the monkey bars to see who is fastest and strongest. Sometimes I win!

Finally, I really like playing tag. My friends and I like to play freeze tag between the soccer goal and the monkey bars. If you get tagged, you have to freeze on the spot. Sometimes we play in partners, so our partners can unfreeze us if they haven't been tagged. Tommy, a boy in my class, is the swiftest runner. It's hard to outrun him when he's it!

So you can see, recess is my favorite time of day. I never get tired of going outside to play!

TLC1058

Learning the Four Square for Narrative Writing

Writing a narrative or imaginative story to a prompt presents another type of challenge. In informational genres, the writer must craft a well-organized explanation or argument on the basis of concrete facts. To construct a narrative, the writer must create all elements of a story: characters, setting, conflict, rise in action, climax, and resolution.

Prepare...

To create, on demand, a story with all necessary elements, a writer must first understand these elements. Gather some narrative/imaginative picture books for study and discussion. Some titles we particularly like include:

<u>Dog Breath</u> by Dav Pilkey

<u>Click Clack Moo</u> by Doreen Cronin

<u>Duck for President</u> by Doreen Cronin

<u>Brave Irene</u> by William Steig

<u>Sylvester and the Magic Pebble</u> by William Steig

<u>The Cat in the Hat</u> by Dr. Seuss

<u>The Hallo Wiener</u> by Dav Pilkey

Any of the <u>Clifford, the Big Red Dog</u> by Norman Bridwell

Any of the <u>Curious George</u> by H. A. and Margret Rey

There is a pattern that exists in many, many popular stories. As readers, we have internalized this pattern and it helps us to organize our thoughts and predictions while reading. This pattern can be represented with a graph of story elements:

Using this graph may be helpful for your visual learners. We'd recommend talking through a few stories, imagining the events that would fall on the slopes of the graph.

Read one of the picture books suggested. Discuss the story elements, and show students the Four Square story graph. Point out that these same elements are in each of the squares of the Four Square (see the **Four Square Narrative Brainstorming Template** on page 22).

Work together to fill in the squares, retelling the story from the picture book. Begin with the character and setting (before the action starts). Continue by placing a phrase to describe the conflict, rise in action, climax and ending in each subsequent square.

Complete the Four Square by adding details in the squares. Hint: Help your students to increase their descriptive writing by adding details about what the characters see, hear, and feel during these events. See the **Four Square Narrative Brainstorming Chart** on page 21.

Placing your students into small groups, distribute one of the recommended picture books to each team. Teams are to read the book together, paying particular attention to characters, setting, conflict, rise in action, climax and ending.

Teams will work together to complete the **Four Square Narrative Brainstorming Template**. You may wish to prepare the template on overhead transparencies to facilitate sharing. After 15-20 minutes, allow teams to share the retelling of their story using the Four Square.

Are your students consistently identifying story elements? Did you observe understanding of these components as the groups worked on the task? If not, repeat this activity as many times as necessary. Understanding story elements is not only good for writing, it is critical for reading comprehension. When you feel like they may be ready, bring on a practice prompt and build your own story!

TLC1058

Four Square for Narrative Writing

Writing a story from a prompt is a daunting task, even for a veteran writer with a thorough understanding of story elements. Modeling the thought process for your students will help them to internalize the detailed thinking that creative writers bring to the page.

Read the prompt to your students and spend a few minutes discussing the possibilities. Chart suggestions for setting, characters, conflict, rise in action, climax and ending:

Prepare...

☐ a chart paper or overhead and appropriate markers

☐ a prompt from our list of practice prompts (see page 42), recycle one of the old assessment prompts, or try one of your own

Setting & Characters	Conflict	Rise in Action	Climax	Ending

If the class cannot form a consensus, YOU choose the story elements and write them on your chart or overhead. Working together is a kooky way to write a story. Remind your students that you want them to see the thinking, but don't expect a prize-winning story in the process!

Call on students to add the "see," "hear," and "feel" details for each story element. Add these to your chart or overhead.

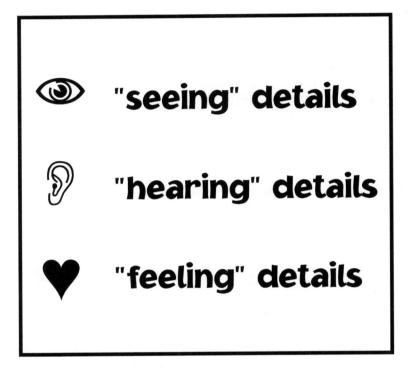

With your chart completed, read your story aloud. Point to the chart elements for the students as you fill in the sentences of your new creation.

Working in teams of 3-4, have students create their own group stories. Assign prompts, or have students choose them randomly from strips of paper in a coffee can. They can complete the brainstorm chart and Four Square on transparencies or chart paper and share with the class.

During group work and sharing, check for evidence of understanding the main story elements. Not there yet? Practice with some more story picture books. Looking solid? Maybe students are ready to tackle some prompts individually.

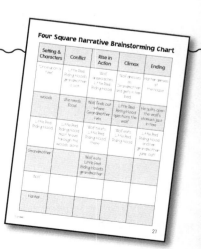

Four Square Narrative Brainstorming Chart

Setting & Characters	Conflict	Rise in Action	Climax	Ending

Four Square Narrative Brainstorming Template

Conflict: _____

_____

_____

👁

👂

♥

Rise in Action: _____

_____

_____

👁

👂

♥

Before the problem: (Setting and Characters)

Who was there?_____

Where were they? _____

When was it? _____

What were they doing? _____

Climax:_____

_____

_____

👁

👂

♥

Ending:_____

_____

_____

👁

👂

♥

TLC10585

Three-Step Revision

On assessment day, our students don't have access to their favorite revision tool: us! Revising independently can be a real challenge. There are actually only four things a writer can do to revise writing:

- add to the draft
- subtract from the draft
- change something around in the draft
- trash it and start over.

On assessment day, we don't recommend the fourth, but you can teach your students to do the first three.

Revising Writing: ADDING

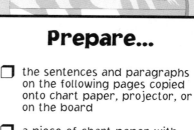

Prepare...

☐ the sentences and paragraphs on the following pages copied onto chart paper, projector, or on the board

☐ a piece of chart paper with the title *Things To add*

☐ make a copy of the **Revising Writing: ADDING Student Practice Page** for each student

We are helping our students to learn some of the things that writers do to add to their writing. Think about the tools writers use to add interest to writing: flashy vocabulary, literary devices, idioms, quotations and more can dress up any student's writing. We'll be working to build an accessible list of things that students can practice adding to writing.

Show students the first sentence on page 24. After reading it aloud, tell your students that you didn't think that the first one was exactly the way you wanted it, so you revised it by ADDING to it!

Reveal the second sentence. Ask students to name what you did to add. *Whatever they tell you is the right answer!* Technically, *chocolate* is an adjective, but any response is accepted.

Chart the student's responses on the *Things to Add* chart (p. 25). Continue with the other sentence examples.

Now we are ready to try this activity with a paragraph. Use the paragraphs on page 27. Ask students to find the added information. Point out that it isn't necessary to add everything, or even to add to every sentence. Can we add other *Things to Add* to our chart?

Student Task

Now your students are ready to try adding to writing. Use the **Revising Writing: ADDING Student Practice Page**. Students should rewrite the sentences and circle what they added (page 26).

Review student responses. Did they find things to add to each sentence? To the paragraph? Write any new ideas on the *Things to Add* chart.

Things to Add
- adjectives
- verbs
- number
-

Revised Writing: ADDING Sentences

The cake was delicious, so I ate it.
The *chocolate* cake was delicious, so I ate it *quickly*.

• • • • • • • •

Grandfather snores.
Grandfather snores *in front of the television every afternoon*.

• • • • • • • •

Today we have no homework.
Today we have no homework *because it is Friday*.

• • • • • • • •

My hands are cold.
My hands are *as* cold *as an iceberg*.

• • • • • • • •

Giovanni loves ice cream.
Giovanni loves *rocky road* ice cream.

• • • • • • • •

Her tummy hurts because she ate candy.
Her tummy hurts because she ate *twelve pieces of* candy.

• • • • • • • •

Mr. Grant is wearing his favorite tie.
Mr. Grant is wearing his favorite *burgundy* tie.

• • • • • • • •

The coach yelled.
The coach yelled, *"Run for it!"*

• • • • • • • •

My mother dropped the pie.
My mother dropped the pie *when she took it out of the oven*.

• • • • • • • •

The pizza looks delicious.
The pizza looks *and smells* delicious.

TLC10585

Things to Add

· · · · · · · · ·

Answers will vary, but these are some possibilities from the ten examples. Chart any responses the students give you, because anything they add is a revision!

Adjectives
Adverbs
What kind?
How?
How many?
Where?
When?
Similes
Color
Size
Dialog
Verbs
Name
Number

Name _____

Revised Writing: ADDING Student Practice Page

Revise the following sentences by ADDING. Write the new sentences on the line, and circle the part you added.

1. I love winter vacation. _____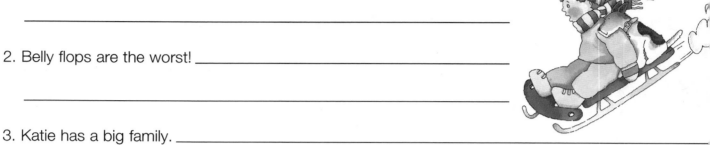

   _____

2. Belly flops are the worst! _____

   _____

3. Katie has a big family. _____

   _____

4. Mrs. Burke is a cool teacher. _____

   _____

5. My birthday was the best. _____

   _____

6. I opened the presents at my party. _____

   _____

7. My dog likes to dig. _____

   _____

8. The bride wore a beautiful gown. _____

   _____

9. Mr. Hampton gave us the envelope. _____

   _____

10. Yesterday I fell down. _____

    _____

TLC10585

Revised Writing: ADDING Paragraphs

There's nothing better than a good piece of cheesecake. I love the creamy taste in my mouth. Cheesecake is my favorite dessert because it's not very sweet. I love the way one part is creamy, and then the crust is crumbly. Sometimes there's a lemony taste, too.

There's nothing better than a good, *cold* piece of cheesecake. I love the creamy taste in my mouth. Cheesecake is my favorite dessert because it's not very sweet, *like ice cream or candy*. I love the way one part is creamy *and smooth*, and then the crust is crumbly. Sometimes there's a *hint of a* lemony taste, too.

• • • • • • • • • • • • • • • • • •

Going to the beach can be a big project. First, you have to dress in swimsuit and shorts. Don't forget your flip flops! The chairs, umbrella, towels and blanket fill up the trunk. Everyone puts on a first coat of sunscreen. We stop to fill the cooler with ice so that our sandwiches and soda pops stay nice and cool. Everyone has things to carry onto the sand until we find our perfect spot.

Going to the beach can be a big project. First, you have to dress in swimsuit and shorts. Don't forget your flip flops! The *reclining beach* chairs, umbrella, towels and blanket fill up the trunk. Everyone puts on a first, *thick* coat of sunscreen. We stop *at the supermarket* to fill the cooler with ice so that our *bologna* sandwiches and soda pops stay nice and cool. Everyone has *five or six* things to carry onto the sand until we find our perfect spot.

ADDING to the Four Square Writing

We've practiced revising by adding as an isolated skill. We've created a chart chock-full of the kinds of adding that your students recognized in the examples and tried on their own. Now we need to apply this to our Four Square Writing!

When we model, we are scaffolding our instruction and giving our students a look at our thought process. We'll model some revising by ADDING to the draft, but then we may need to remove our example. Some students may wish to copy our adding instead of trying it on their own!

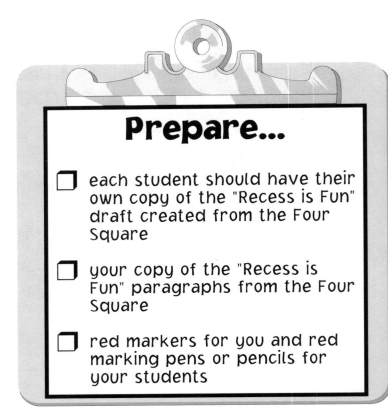

Prepare...

☐ each student should have their own copy of the "Recess is Fun" draft created from the Four Square

☐ your copy of the "Recess is Fun" paragraphs from the Four Square

☐ red markers for you and red marking pens or pencils for your students

Read through your class's "Recess is Fun" draft, and identify places where you can add a detail. Is there a place where you could add adjectives, adverbs, what kind, how, how many, where, when, similes, color, size, dialog, verbs, names or numbers? Remember, we are not looking to do ALL of these. Let's begin by adding ONE thing.

Remember, there is NO WRONG ANSWER. Anything you add is correct.

Model for your students with the red marking pencil. Show the + sign in the margin, and then use a caret (rooftop) to insert the idea.

TLC10585

Each with their own copy of "Recess is Fun," have your students read the paper and find ONE PLACE to add ONE THING. Using their red marking pencils, students should indicate the + sign in the margin and the caret or rooftop with the added information. As you call on students, discuss and praise all the things your students have added. Are there more *Things to Add* to your chart? Put them up there!

Things to Add
- adjectives
- verbs
- number
-

First of all, playing on the swings is the best. My friend Judy and I take turns on the swings. She's bigger than I am, so she pushes me way up high. The wind whooshes past my face and sometimes I see birds flying by me. When my turn ends, I jump off in mid-air and
+ land ^ in the dirt in a cloud of dust.
   with a plop

Are your students adding information? Details? Can you nudge your strong writers to add similes or figurative language? Are your struggling writers able to find a place to add a name, number, or adjective?

Revised Writing: SUBTRACTING

Sometimes our strongest writers can be a bit over-zealous in their first drafts, making them chatty and full of extra words. We can learn to look for certain "extras" and subtract them to make our writing more succinct. Remind your students, when prac-ticing subtraction we ~~cross out~~ and never erase! Erasing takes too long, makes a messy paper, and destroys the record of what we had before.

We are helping our students learn some of the things that writers do to tidy up their writing. Think about the kinds of wordiness we see in student writing. The *really*, *very*, *a lot*, and filler words stu-dents use can often be subtracted. We'll be work-ing to build an accessible list of things that students can practice subtracting from writing.

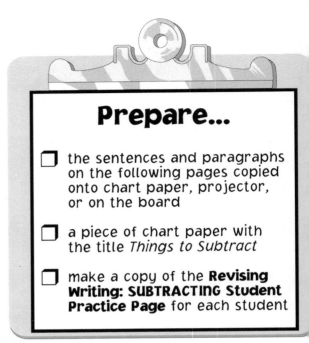

Prepare...

- [ ] the sentences and paragraphs on the following pages copied onto chart paper, projector, or on the board

- [ ] a piece of chart paper with the title *Things to Subtract*

- [ ] make a copy of the **Revising Writing: SUBTRACTING Student Practice Page** for each student

Show students the first sentence on page 31. After reading it aloud, tell your students that you didn't think that the first one was exactly th[e] way you wanted it, so you revised it by SUBTRACTING from it!

Reveal the second sentence. Ask students to name what you sub-tracted. *Whatever they tell you is the right answer!* Technically, *around and around* was repetition, but any response is accepted!

Chart the student's responses on the *Things to Subtract* chart (p. 32[)]. Continue with the other sentence examples.

Now we are ready to try this activity with a paragraph. Use the para-graphs on page 34. Ask students to find the subtracted information. Point out that it isn't necessary to subtract everything, or even to sub[-]tract from every sentence. Can we add other *Things to Subtract* to o[ur] chart?

Now your students are ready to try subtracting from writ-ing. Use the **Revising Writing: SUBTRACTING Student Practice Page** (p. 33). Students should cross out the extra words and rewrite the sentence.

Review student responses. Did they find things to subtract from each sentence? From the paragraph? Write any new ideas on the *Things to Subtract* chart.

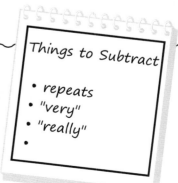

Things to Subtract

- repeats
- "very"
- "really"
-

TLC10585

Revised Writing: SUBTRACTING Sentences

My dog was scared by the snake, so he was running circles around and around the yard.

My dog was scared by the snake, so he was running circles around ~~and around~~ the yard.

• • • • • • • •

The white and fluffy snow was so beautiful, cold, and fluffy white when it fell out of the very cloudy sky on that cold and very stormy day.

The white and fluffy snow was so beautiful, ~~cold, and fluffy white~~ when it fell ~~out of the very cloudy sky~~ on that cold and ~~very~~ stormy day.

• • • • • • • •

That party was so very, very fun because we did the most fun activities like playing a fun and awesome game of flashlight tag.

That party was ~~so very, very~~ fun because we did ~~the most fun~~ activities like playing ~~a fun~~ and awesome game of flashlight tag.

• • • • • • • •

The beautiful yellow sun was shining so very brightly that I thought it would be a great and very wonderful day for an awesome and fantastic picnic.

The ~~beautiful yellow~~ sun was shining so ~~very~~ brightly that I thought it would be a great ~~and very wonderful~~ day for a~~n~~ ~~awesome and fantastic~~ picnic.

• • • • • • • •

The pizza burned my mouth when I ate it.

The pizza burned my mouth ~~when I ate it~~.

• • • • • • • •

My nice mother makes us some awesome and great pancakes when we have our huge and gigantic breakfast on Sunday.

My ~~nice~~ mother makes us ~~some awesome and~~ great pancakes when we have our huge ~~and gigantic~~ breakfast on Sunday.

Things to Subtract

· · · · · · · ·

Answers will vary, but these are some possibilities from the six examples. Chart any responses the students give you, because anything they add is a revision!

Repetitions

Redundancies

Obvious Things

"Really"

"A lot"

"So"

"Very"

TLC10585

Revised Writing: SUBTRACTING Student Practice Page

Revise the following sentences by SUBTRACTING. ~~Cross through~~ the extra words and then rewrite the new sentences on the line.

1. My really lazy cats like to lie around all day. _____

_____

2. My shoes really hurt when I wear them. _____

_____

3. The weather was cold so I was, like, freezing. _____

_____

4. The dark sky was very dark at midnight. _____

_____

5. My really nice art teacher let us have free choice in art class today. _____

_____

6. The mall was so very crowded and full of people. _____

_____

7. Emily likes to talk and talk a lot when we ride the bus to school. _____

_____

8. The really loud rock concert hurt my ears because it was so very loud. _____

_____

9. Yesterday in the afternoon on the way home from school Michael fell off his bike when he was riding it.

_____

_____

10. The green grass looked so soft and fluffy when the yellow sun was shining so very brightly.

_____

_____

Revised Writing: SUBTRACTING Paragraphs

Sometimes I like to have a tangy and tart piece of grapefruit. This is a treat that is really very sweet and sour when I taste it in my mouth. To make it better, I sometimes put a scoop of sweet sugar on the top. It is really a very healthy and good for you snack when you eat it!

Sometimes I like to have a tangy ~~and tart~~ piece of grapefruit. This is a treat that is ~~really very~~ sweet and sour ~~when I taste it~~ in my mouth. To make it better, I sometimes put a scoop of ~~sweet~~ sugar on the top. It is ~~really~~ a very healthy and good for you snack ~~when you eat it~~!

· · · · · · · · · · · · · · · · · · · ·

Every Sunday during football season, my family really likes to watch a lot of football on TV when it is on. We all sit on the very big and comfortable couch in the family room. My very nice mother makes us some delicious and yummy snacks. She makes extremely spicy and hot chicken wings. I like to dip them into the creamy and smooth white ranch dressing. The game comes on and we all yell and cheer very loud when our very favorite team scores in the game.

Every Sunday during football season, my family ~~really~~ likes to watch a lot of football on TV ~~when it is on~~. We all sit on the ~~very big and~~ comfortable couch in the family room. My ~~very nice~~ mother makes us some ~~delicious and~~ yummy snacks. She makes extremely spicy ~~and hot~~ chicken wings. I like to dip them into the creamy and smooth ~~white~~ ranch dressing. The game comes on and we all yell ~~and cheer very loud~~ when our ~~very~~ favorite team scores ~~in the game~~.

34

TLC10585

SUBTRACTING from the Four Square Writing

Now we've practiced revising by SUBTRACTING as an isolated skill. We've created a chart chock-full of the kinds of subtracting that your students recognized in the examples and tried on their own. Now we need to apply this to our Four Square Writing!

When we model, we are scaffolding our instruction and giving our students a look at our thought process. We'll model some revising by SUBTRACTING from the draft, but then we may need to remove our example. Some students may wish to copy our subtracting instead of trying it on their own!

Read through your class's "Recess is Fun" draft, and find a place where we may be able to SUBTRACT some information. For example, in our third paragraph:

Prepare...

☐ each student should have their own copy of the "Recess is Fun" draft created from the Four Square

☐ your copy of the "Recess is Fun" paragraphs from the Four Square

☐ red markers for you and red marking pens or pencils for your students

---

Also, the monkey bars are always lots of fun. I like to pretend I'm Tarzan and give that yell, "AHHHHHHHYYYYYYYEEEEEEE!" I swing hand over hand across the top of the overhanging ladder and imagine I'm swinging over a rushing river. Sometimes my friends and I race all the way to the top of the monkey bars to see who is fastest and strongest. Sometimes I win!

Couldn't we delete like this without changing the meaning?

Also, the monkey bars are always lots of fun. I like to pretend I'm Tarzan and give that yell, "AHHHHHHHYYYYYYYEEEEEEE!" I swing hand over hand across the top of the overhanging
− ladder and imagine I'm ~~swinging~~ over a rushing river. Sometimes my friends and I race all the way to the top of the monkey bars to see who is fastest and strongest. Sometimes I win!

Or like this?

− Also, the monkey bars are always ~~lots of~~ fun. I like to pretend I'm Tarzan and give that yell, "AHHHHHHHYYYYYYYEEEEEEE!" I swing hand over hand across the top of the overhanging ladder and imagine I'm swinging over a rushing river. Sometimes my friends and I race all the way to the top of the monkey bars to see who is fastest and strongest. Sometimes I win!

Show your students how you indicate the SUBTRACTION with the red marking pencil, striking through the information once. NEVER erase. Indicate the subtraction with the − sign in the margin.

Student Task

Each with their own copy of "Recess is Fun," have your students read the paper and decide ONE PLACE to subtract ONE THING. Using their red marking pencils, students should indicate the − sign in the margin and strikethrough the subtracted information. As you call on students, discuss and praise all the things your students have subtracted. Are there more *Things to Subtract* for your chart? Put them up there!

Things to Subtract

• repeats
• "very"
• "really"
•

Revised Writing: CHANGING

We often put things in a first draft just for the sake of getting our ideas on the page. The purpose of revising is to look over the writing and see it again. Now we may see some things that can be changed!

We are helping our students to learn some of the things that writers do to add to their writing. Think about the tools writers use to add interest to writing: flashy vocabulary, literary devices, idioms, quotations and more can dress up any student's writing. We'll be working to build an accessible list of things that students can practice changing in their writing.

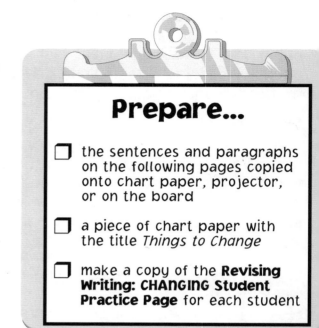

Prepare...

☐ the sentences and paragraphs on the following pages copied onto chart paper, projector, or on the board

☐ a piece of chart paper with the title *Things to Change*

☐ make a copy of the **Revising Writing: CHANGING Student Practice Page** for each student

Show students the first sentence on page 37. After reading it aloud, tell your students that you didn't think that the first one was exactly the way you wanted it, so you revised it by CHANGING it!

Reveal the second sentence. Ask students to name what you did to change. *Whatever they tell you is the right answer!*

Chart the student's responses on the *Things to Change* chart (p. 38) Continue with the other sentence examples.

Now we are ready to try this activity with a paragraph. Use the paragraphs on page 40. Ask students to find the changed information. Point out that it isn't necessary to change everything, or even to change every sentence. Can we add other *Things to Change* to our chart?

Student Task

Now your students are ready to try changing writing. Use the **Revising Writing: CHANGING Student Practice Page** (p. 39). Students should rewrite the sentence and circle what they changed.

Review student responses. Did they find things to change in each sentence? To the paragraph? Write any new ideas on the *Things to Change* chart.

Things to Change

• combine sentences
• stronger verbs
• more specific
•

TLC10585

Revised Writing: CHANGING Sentences

My friend Barb is funny.
My friend Barb keeps us laughing with her non-stop jokes.

• • • • • • • •

The cats play.
The naughty kittens make a game out of everything.

• • • • • • • •

My sandwich was delicious.
My BLT tasted like heaven on Earth.

• • • • • • • •

The flowers smelled good.
The roses smelled like perfume.

• • • • • • • •

I did my homework after I watched TV.
After I watched TV, I did my homework.

• • • • • • • •

Geoffrey ran two laps. Then he threw the football.
Geoffrey ran two laps, then threw the football.

• • • • • • • •

Erin talks and talks in class.
Erin never stops yapping in class.

• • • • • • • •

That meal was very large.
That meal was a belt-buster.

• • • • • • • •

Eric and Jonathan and Emma and Hayden and D'Jenne
waited for me.
A bunch of my friends waited for me.

• • • • • • • •

The coffee was hot.
The coffee was an inferno.

Things to Change

• • • • • • • •

Answers will vary, but these are some possibilities from the ten examples. Chart any responses the students give you, because anything they add is a revision!

Stronger verbs

Specific words

Similes

Word order

Combining sentences

Make things clearer

Tell how many

Name _____

Revised Writing: CHANGING Student Practice Page

Revise the following sentences by CHANGING. Write the new sentences on the line, and circle the change.

1. I fell down and scraped my knee at recess. _____

_____

2. For dessert, we had some sweets. _____

_____

3. I danced to some music this morning. _____

_____

4. I had to go to the store over the weekend. _____

_____

5. The kids looked tired after the long soccer practice. _____

_____

6. I screamed when I jumped in the pool, because the water was cold. _____

_____

7. My little brother made a mess with his spaghetti. _____

_____

8. Uncle Edwin always brings us great presents. _____

_____

9. I was happy when I got a great present for my birthday. _____

_____

10. My friends came over and we all played a game. _____

_____

Revised Writing: CHANGING Paragraphs

I like to go for a run every morning. I wake up very early. I don't like getting out of bed when it is still dark out, but I do it. I am out the door by 5:30. I am on the street in the dark. I run a five-mile loop. I come home and shower. I feel better when I start my day with exercise.

I enjoy my daily morning run, even though I wake up very early. Getting out of bed when it is still dark can be painful, but I do it. Out the door by 5:30 and on the dark streets, I run a five-mile loop before I come home and shower. Starting my day with exercise makes me feel better.

• • • • • • • • • • • • • • • • • • •

My family goes for a picnic on Fathers' Day every year. We meet at a cool state park. All the cousins come. There are tons of kids. We eat all day long. The aunts all make their special foods. The kids play. We all toast marshmallows when it gets dark. I always fall asleep on the way home.

Every year my family goes for a Father's Day picnic. We meet at Running River State park, which has boat rentals, hiking trails, tennis courts and a fabulous playground. All the cousins come, even the cousins who live all the way in New Jersey. There are more than thirty kids. All day long, we are snacking on the special foods the aunts make. We have casseroles, salads, sweet treats, and Aunt Darlene's famous banana pudding. The kids run wild in the park. When it gets dark we all toast marshmallows. On the way home, I always fall asleep.

• • • • • • • • • • • • • • • • • • •

Don't even talk to my dad before he has had his coffee. He is in a bad mood. He will not be nice to us. He usually has two cups while we are watching cartoons on Saturday morning. He drinks it black and strong. He never adds sugar. After his coffee he is back to being my awesome dad.

Don't talk to Dad! He hasn't had his coffee! Before his coffee, he's in a bad mood and will not be nice to us. On Saturday morning, Dad usually has two cups while we are watching cartoons. He drinks it black, strong, and never adds sugar. After coffee, he is back to being my awesome dad.

TLC10585

CHANGING the Four Square Writing

Now we've practiced revising by CHANGING as an isolated skill. We've created a chart chock-full of the kinds of changing that your students recognized in the examples and tried on their own. Now we need to apply this to our Four Square Writing!

When we model, we are scaffolding our instruction and giving our students a look at our thought process. We'll model some revising by CHANGING from the draft, but then we may need to remove our example. Some students may wish to copy our changing instead of trying it on their own!

Read through your class's "Recess is Fun" draft, and find ONE PLACE to change ONE THING. For example, in our fourth paragraph:

Prepare...

☐ each student should have their own copy of the "Recess is Fun" draft created from the Four Square

☐ your copy of the "Recess is Fun" paragraphs from the Four Square

☐ red markers for you and red marking pens or pencils for your students

Finally, I really like playing tag. My friends and I like to play freeze tag between the soccer goal and the monkey bars. If you get tagged, you have to freeze on the spot. Sometimes we play in partners, so our partners can unfreeze us if they haven't been tagged. Tommy, a boy in my class, is the swiftest runner. It's hard to outrun him when he's it!

Maybe we could change it like this:

C Finally, I **could spend every day** playing tag. My friends and I like to play freeze tag between the soccer goal and the monkey bars. If you get tagged, you have to freeze on the spot. Sometimes we play in partners, so our partners can unfreeze us if they haven't been tagged. Tommy, a boy in my class, is the swiftest runner. It's hard to outrun him when he's it!

Or, maybe like this:

Finally, I really like playing tag. My friends and I like to play freeze tag between the soccer goal and the monkey bars. If you get tagged, you have to freeze on the spot. Sometimes we play in partners so our partners can unfreeze us if they C haven't been tagged. Tommy, a boy in my class, **runs like a gazelle.** It's hard to outrun him when he's it!

Show your students how you indicate the CHANGE with the red marking pencil, striking through the information once, and indicating the change above the original. NEVER erase. Indicate the change with a *C* in the margin.

Student Task

Each with their own copy of "Recess is Fun," have your students read the paper and decide ONE PLACE to change ONE THING. Using their red marking pencils, students should indicate the *C* in the margin and a strikethrough and insert for the information. As you call on students, discuss and praise all the things your students have changed. Are there more *Things to Change* for your chart? Put them up there! Are your students changing information? Can you nudge your strongest writers to change using figurative language and strong verbs?

Things to Change

• combine sentences
• stronger verbs
• more specific
•

Prompts for Practicing

Expository Prompts

1. Our lives are full of important people such as family and friends. Who are some of the people important to you? Choose one important person and explain why they are special to you.

2. Everyone has favorite memories. Think of a memory that is very special to you. Write to explain why that memory is special.

3. Holidays can be special times. Think of a holiday that was memorable to you. Write to explain that holiday memory.

4. Everyone is afraid of something—the dark, the boogeyman, or snakes. What scares you? Write about what you fear and how you face that fear.

5. What are some of your favorite activities outside of school? Do you like sports or arts and crafts? Write about one favorite hobby and explain why you enjoy it.

6. Many people love sunny days, but rainy days come, too. How do you spend your time on a rainy day? Write to explain how rainy days can be just as fun as sunny days.

7. We all have our strengths and weaknesses. Think of something you do particularly well. Write to explain what you do and how you are so good at doing it.

8. Many people have a place they like to be. What is your favorite place? Write to describe your place and explain why you like to be there.

9. Some people are morning people and others are night owls. What time of day do you like? Write to explain what you do and why you like that particular time of day.

10. Monday is the first school day of the week, and Friday signals the week's end. Saturday and Sunday are days for catching up, having fun, and family time. Which day is your favorite? Explain why you like this day and what you enjoy doing on your favorite day of the week.

TLC10585

11. Good advice is hard to find, even though we can get advice from many sources. What is the best advice you have ever gotten? Write about that advice and explain why it was the best.

- -

12. Birthdays give us a chance to wish for celebrations and gifts. What is the best birthday gift you could imagine getting? Explain the gift and why it would be the best.

- -

13. In history and in current events, we learn about important and heroic people. Who do you admire? Write about that person and explain why you admire him or her.

- -

14. There are many reasons for celebrations. Maybe your team won a championship, or you just got your braces off. Think of the best celebration you've ever had. Write to explain why that was the best celebration.

- -

15. Some of us have many friends who are close to us, but one that is very special. Who is your best friend? Write to explain why that person is so important to you.

- -

16. Some relatives are in our houses and neighborhoods, so we see them often. Others live far away and we see them rarely. Think of a favorite relative, far or near, and explain why that relative is a favorite.

- -

17. A new student arrives at your school and needs your help. Write to explain how you would help a new student at your school.

- -

18. Saving up money for something is hard, especially for a kid. If you needed some cash, how would you earn extra money? Write your plan for earning some money of your own.

- -

19. Taking care of the earth is everybody's responsibility. Sure, students can't clean up toxic waste sites by themselves. But what can they do? Write to explain how kids can help the environment.

- -

20. Three- and four-year-old kids can be a handful. Some are jumpy bundles of energy. Think about the way preschoolers act, and imagine it is your job to take care of one. Write to explain how you would entertain a small child.

Narrative Prompts

1. You are enjoying your morning glass of orange juice when you notice something unusual. You can fly! Write about your life with your new power.

2. One morning you awaken and look in the mirror, only to see nothing where your reflection should be. You are invisible! Write a story about your invisible life.

3. Some animals live in our homes, while others live in the zoo or in the wild. Which animal would you like to be? Choose one and explain why you'd most like to live the life of that animal.

4. There are many choices when it comes to snack foods, but we don't always choose wisely. Think about all the junk foods many kids like to eat, and the problems they could cause. Write to explain why it is important to choose healthy snacks.

5. Different weather makes for different activities. Write a story about a day in which the weather made for a special day. Tell what happened on this day.

6. We can set goals for all kinds of personal achievements. Think of a time when you set a goal and reached it. Tell the story of how it happened, and provide details of how you felt while reaching your goal.

7. Starting school is a frightening time for many young children. What do you remember about your first day of school? Write about that first day, including details about your memories of that first experience.

8. Superheroes in the comic strips often have some wonderful powers such as x-ray vision, the ability to fly, or super-human strength. Imagine that you wake up one morning and find that you are a superhero or heroine and have one power to use for a day. Write about your adventurous day with this super power.

9. Movie stars live in Hollywood, or maybe in another far-away place. But what if your favorite movie star came to your neighborhood? Write a story about the time you met your favorite movie star.

10. You woke up during the night and saw some strange lights out your window. There was flashing and color that you had never seen before. Write a story about what happened on the night with the flashing lights.

44

11. Sometimes it seems like everything went wrong. Have you ever had a day like that? Write a story about a time you had a bad day.

- -

12. If we look carefully in the world around us, there are treasures to be had. Write a story about a time you found something special to you.

- -

13. With books, papers, and supplies, there are so many things to keep track of that sometimes things get lost. Write a story about a time you lost something.

- -

14. Field trips can be some of the best memories from school. They give us a chance to get out in the world and explore learning with our classmates. Write about a time you went on a field trip.

- -

15. Surprise parties can be wonderful, but not every surprise is a good one. Write a story about a time you were surprised.

- -

16. Friends are there for good times and bad times. Think about a time a friend had a problem, and you were there. Write a story about how you helped that friend.

- -

17. Sometimes a storm knocks down the power lines. Sometimes the lights go out and we don't know why. How would your life be different without electricity? Write a story about a time you had to spend the day without electrical power.

- -

18. A bad cold can take your voice away. If it hasn't happened to you, imagine how hard life would be if you couldn't talk. Write a story about a day you couldn't speak.

- -

19. Waking up one morning, you realize you are only 3 inches tall! Write a story about your day as a tiny person.

- -

20. As we grow, we learn, and the learning continues even as we get older. Think about a time you learned something new. Write a story about how you learned it.

Persuasive Prompts

1. The right to drive a car is anticipated eagerly by most teenagers. What would you think if the legislature decided to raise the driving age to 21? Write a persuasive paper for or against this idea.

- -

2. Hunting is a hobby that raises many controversies. What do you think of this hobby? Should it be protected or banned? Write to support your position.

- -

3. Some professional athletes make millions of dollars a year playing their sport. Do you think this is fair, considering that police officers, teachers, and other community members make barely a fraction of that?

- -

4. It is a good idea to get to bed at a reasonable hour on school nights, but sometimes we want to stay up on a Friday. Write to persuade your parents to let you stay up super late on a Friday night.

- -

5. You want to go see this new movie, but your friend isn't sure. Write to persuade your friend to go catch this new movie with you.

- -

6. Skate parks are places where kids can practice their moves without having to worry about cars and traffic, but they are expensive to build. Write to your legislators to persuade them to build a skate park in your neighborhood.

- -

7. Pets provide great company but they are a big responsibility. Write to persuade your parents to get you a dog, cat, or other animal.

- -

8. Cell phones can be used for communication, for fun, and for emergencies, but they can be expensive. Write to persuade your parents to get you a cell phone of your very own.

- -

9. Many kids earn an allowance by helping out with chores or other household duties. Do you get an allowance? Do you think it is enough? Write to persuade your parents to start or to increase your allowance.

- -

10. Technology changes quickly, and the best work requires the best tools. Do you have a computer? Do you need a new and improved one? Write to persuade your parents to buy you a new computer.

TLC1058

11. The rainforest is still in danger of being overrun by modern developments. Many times elected officials can use their influence to help issues that are important to you. Write to persuade an elected official that saving the rainforest requires his or her support.

- -

12. With a busy school day, sometimes recess is the thing that is forgotten or cut. What can be done? Write to persuade your teacher to give you extra recess during the day.

- -

13. Sometimes the relatives we love have terrible habits. Some of these habits may be unhealthy but very hard to break. Think about what you know about the dangers of smoking. Write to persuade your relative to give up smoking.

- -

14. Sometimes the relatives we love have unhealthy habits. Not exercising enough or overeating is a habit many people have. Think about what you know about the dangers of being overweight. Write to persuade your relative to start exercising.

- -

15. A special book can excite us for many reasons. It can become a favorite that you want all your friends to read for themselves. Think about a book you enjoyed. Write to persuade a friend to read this book.

- -

16. Hobbies are very personal and very enjoyable. Think about a hobby or activity you enjoy. Write to persuade a friend to try this activity.

- -

17. Many people have that one TV program that they just can't miss. Think about a show you enjoy. Write to persuade a friend to watch this show.

- -

18. Many school boards have decided on a school uniform policy for all students. What do you think of school uniforms? Would you like them or not? Write to the school board to persuade them to vote for or against such a policy.

- -

19. Visiting relatives can be fun, but the fun can be even better if a friend comes along. Think about a relative you enjoy visiting. Write to persuade a friend to join you on your visit.

- -

20. Most kids like free choice day at PE, when students have a chance to decide which activities they like doing. Write to persuade your PE teacher to let your class have a free choice day in PE.

About the Authors

Judith S. Gould

Judy is a teacher, writer and educational speaker who has been sharing ideas for writing success in schools nationwide. She has taught nearly all grades, including Pre-K and high school. When at home in Florida, she enjoys reading and writing with husband Evan, daughter Ilana and Figaro the cat.

Mary F. Burke

Mary has been a teacher for 23 years. She is currently the writing teacher at Jacksonville Beach Elementary in Florida. She enjoys writing poetry and having a simple life with her husband Cal and her dog, Mel and cat, Ripley.

48